Queen Esther Saves Her People

RETOLD BY RITA GOLDEN GELMAN

ILLUSTRATED BY FRANÉ LESSAC

SCHOLASTIC PRESS • NEW YORK

For David Barr, who gave so much to so many.
—RITA GOLDEN GELMAN

For my grandmother Esther.
—FRANÉ LESSAC

AUTHOR'S NOTE: The menorah that appears on page 9 has the seven candlesticks appropriate to the time of the First Temple.

ARTIST'S NOTE: The Hebrew text on the decorative "scrolls" found on pages 20-21 is taken from the Book of Esther.

LIBRARY OF CONGRESS CATALOGING-IN-PUBLICATION DATA

Gelman, Rita Golden.
Queen Esther saves her people / Rita Golden Gelman ; with illustrations by Frané Lessac. p. cm.
Summary: Retells the story of how a beautiful Jewish girl became the Queen of Persia and saved her people from death at the hands of the evil Hamen.
ISBN 0-590-47025-6
1. Esther, Queen of Persia—Juvenile literature. 2. Bible stories, English—O.T. Esther. [1. Esther, Queen of Persia. 2. Bible stories—O.T. 3. Purim.] I. Lessac, Frané, ill. II. Title.   BS580.E8G45   1998
222'.909505—dc21   97-2568   CIP AC

2 4 6 8 10 9 7 5 3 1
8 9/9 0/0 01 02 03

Printed in U.S.A.   37
First edition, February 1998

The pictures in this book were created using gouache.
The text was set in Cooper Old Style.
Book design by Marijka Kostiw.

The Book of Esther

is a Bible story that takes place more than

twenty-five hundred years ago in the city of

Shushan in the ancient Persian Empire. It is a story

of good and evil, of caring and callousness, and of

the extraordinary courage of one young woman.

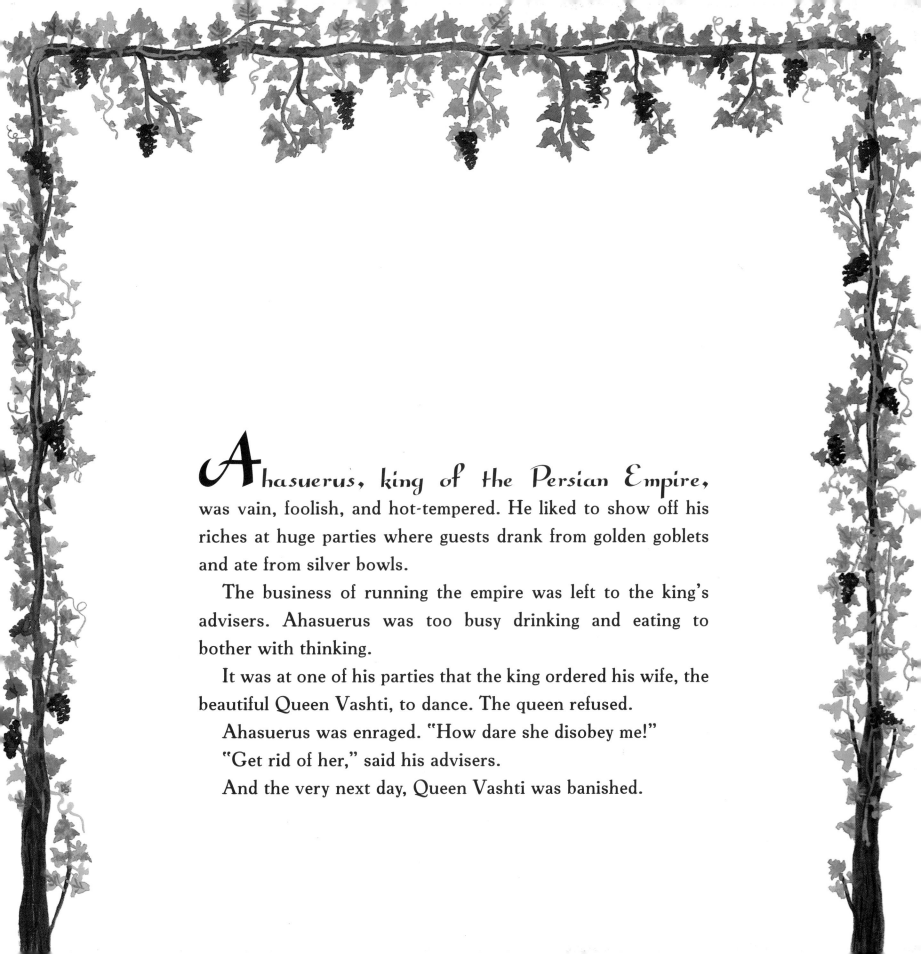

$\mathcal{A}$hasuerus, king of the Persian Empire, was vain, foolish, and hot-tempered. He liked to show off his riches at huge parties where guests drank from golden goblets and ate from silver bowls.

The business of running the empire was left to the king's advisers. Ahasuerus was too busy drinking and eating to bother with thinking.

It was at one of his parties that the king ordered his wife, the beautiful Queen Vashti, to dance. The queen refused.

Ahasuerus was enraged. "How dare she disobey me!"

"Get rid of her," said his advisers.

And the very next day, Queen Vashti was banished.

Days, weeks, months went by. Ahasuerus grew lonely and very bad-tempered. He missed Queen Vashti.

"He will punish us for what happened to the queen," said one of his advisers.

"He will hang us," said another.

"But not if we find him a new queen who is even more beautiful than Vashti," said a third.

The search began. Beautiful young women arrived at the palace from all over the empire.

Now there was in the city of Shushan, not far from the palace, a beautiful young woman named Esther. She lived with her cousin Mordecai, for both of her parents had died when she was a baby.

Esther and Mordecai lived in Persia, but they were not Persian; they were Jewish. Many years before they were born, their ancestors had been taken prisoner by the king of Persia and brought to his country.

By the time Ahasuerus became king, the Jews were no longer prisoners. They spoke Persian and dressed like their Persian neighbors. They lived by the laws of their new land. They bought and sold in the market. They even served in the king's army. But in their homes, they practiced the Jewish religion.

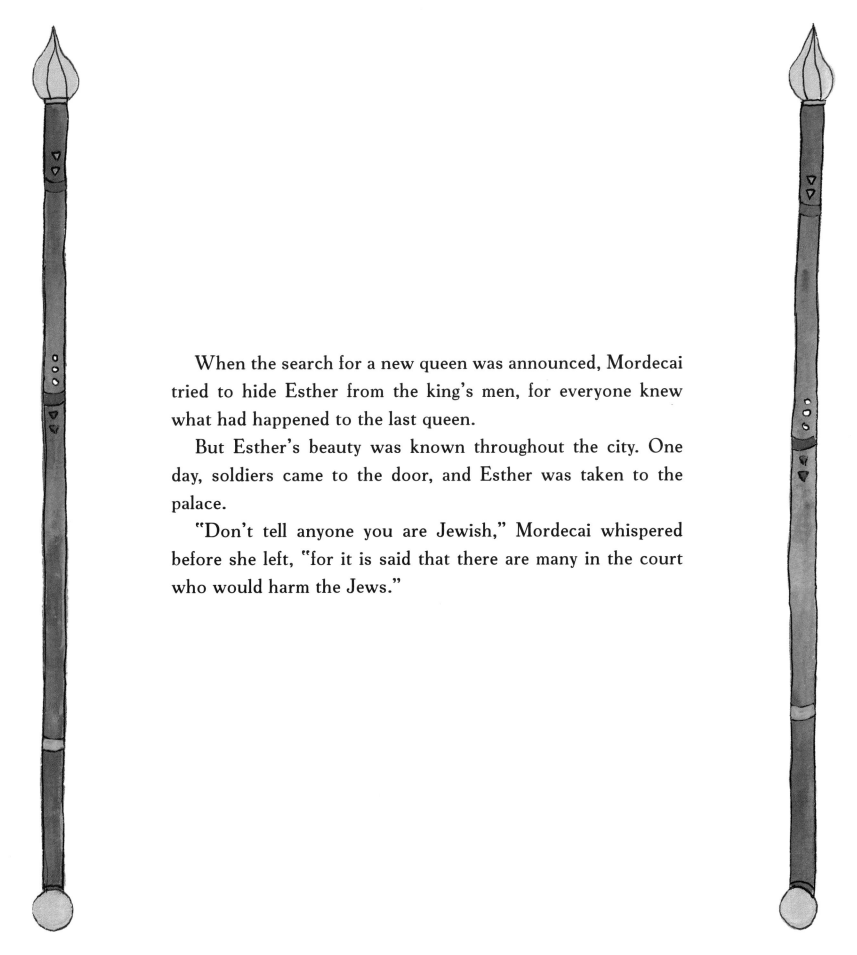

When the search for a new queen was announced, Mordecai tried to hide Esther from the king's men, for everyone knew what had happened to the last queen.

But Esther's beauty was known throughout the city. One day, soldiers came to the door, and Esther was taken to the palace.

"Don't tell anyone you are Jewish," Mordecai whispered before she left, "for it is said that there are many in the court who would harm the Jews."

Inside the palace walls, Esther lived in a special house with the other young women.

For one year they were massaged with fragrant oils and sprinkled with exotic perfumes. Their hair was brushed. Their nails were clipped. Their lips were painted. Their cheeks were blushed. All this was to prepare them to meet the king.

The young women spoke many languages. They were of many religions. And they were all beautiful, each in her own way.

Esther enjoyed meeting women from many different parts of the empire. But she missed Mordecai, for she was not allowed to leave the palace grounds, and he was not allowed to enter.

Each day Mordecai walked past the women's courtyard and looked inside so that he would know how his cousin was doing.

One by one, day after day, the women were brought to the king. And one by one, day after day, he rejected them all.

Finally, it was Esther's turn. Though she was offered robes that sparkled with gold, and necklaces that radiated with diamonds, Esther chose to wear a simple white dress. When she entered the king's chambers, it was her natural beauty that sparkled and radiated.

The king was overwhelmed. He placed the royal crown on her head and proclaimed her Queen Esther.

Mordecai missed his cousin. He spent many hours sitting near the gateway to the palace, where servants of the king and queen would gather and gossip. There, he would listen for news about Esther.

One day, Mordecai overheard two servants plotting to kill the king. He immediately sent a message to Esther, and Esther told the king.

The servants were hanged on a tree.

Later, the story of the assassination plot and Mordecai's warning was recorded in the king's diary.

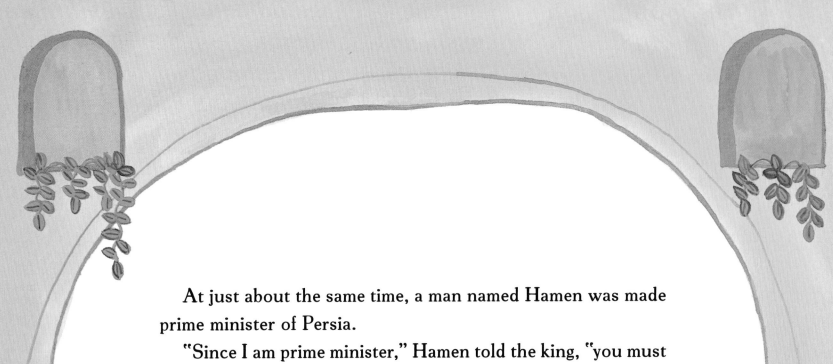

At just about the same time, a man named Hamen was made prime minister of Persia.

"Since I am prime minister," Hamen told the king, "you must order everyone to bow down before me."

The king, of course, did what he was told.

Wherever Hamen went, people bowed, but Mordecai refused.

"I am a Jew," said Mordecai, "and Jews do not bow down to human beings."

Whenever Hamen walked through the palace gate, he saw Mordecai standing while everyone else bowed.

He insults me, thought Hamen. I will have him killed. And with him, every Jew in Persia. Thousands will die because Mordecai is a fool.

That night, Hamen chose a day, twelve months later, when all the Jews would die.

The next morning the king was playing cards when Hamen arrived.

"Sire," said Hamen. "There are certain people scattered throughout the empire whose ways are different from the rest of the people and they refuse to obey your laws. You must decree that they all be killed . . . men, women, and children. I have chosen the thirteenth day of the month of Adar for the killings."

"You may do whatever you like," said the king, distractedly, and he went back to playing his game.

Because of the evil mind of Hamen and the empty mind of the king, all of the Jews in Persia were sentenced to die.

When Jews throughout the empire heard the news, they wept and wailed and mourned.

Queen Esther, sheltered inside the palace walls, never even heard about the decree until Mordecai sent her a message. "You must plead with the king to save your people," he told her.

Esther trembled when she heard what Mordecai was asking. No one, not even the queen, was permitted to approach the king unless he called for her. The penalty was death.

Esther sent a message back to Mordecai.

"I am afraid," she said. "I have not even seen the king for thirty days."

"You cannot think about yourself," he responded. "It is possible that you have been put on the throne for this very moment. You must go."

For three days Esther fasted and prayed. And all the Jews of Shushan fasted and prayed with her. On the third day, she walked toward the king's courtyard.

If I die, I die, she thought.

There was a hush when the courtiers saw the queen enter.

The king looked at Queen Esther. He saw another queen defying his rules, risking death, but instead of becoming angry, he welcomed her.

"What is it you wish, Queen Esther?" he asked.

"If it is to your liking, my king, I invite you and Hamen to come today to a banquet I have prepared."

The king turned to his servants. "See that Hamen makes himself ready," he ordered.

Esther and her guests wined and dined in elegance.

When the last dessert was eaten, the king asked again, "What is it you wish, Queen Esther? Whatever it is, you shall have it . . . even if it is half of the kingdom."

Esther began to speak, but the words would not come.

"For now," she said, "I ask only that you and Hamen come back again tomorrow for another banquet. I will tell you then what it is that I wish."

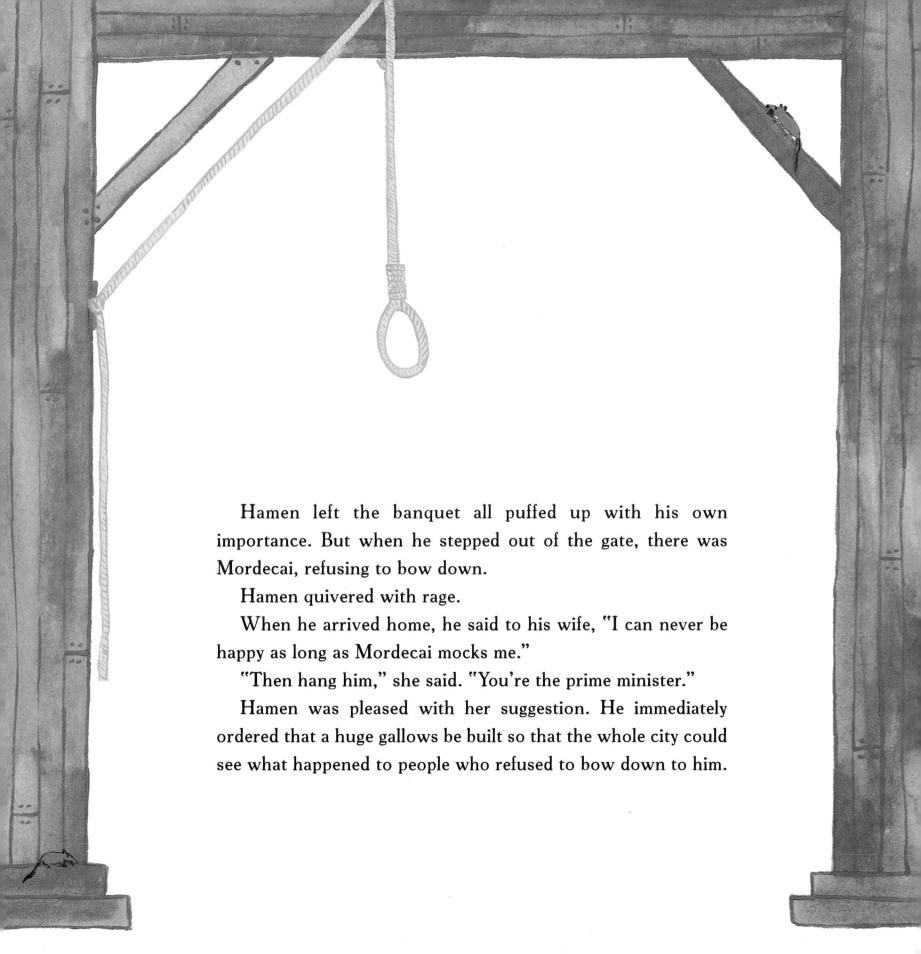

Hamen left the banquet all puffed up with his own importance. But when he stepped out of the gate, there was Mordecai, refusing to bow down.

Hamen quivered with rage.

When he arrived home, he said to his wife, "I can never be happy as long as Mordecai mocks me."

"Then hang him," she said. "You're the prime minister."

Hamen was pleased with her suggestion. He immediately ordered that a huge gallows be built so that the whole city could see what happened to people who refused to bow down to him.

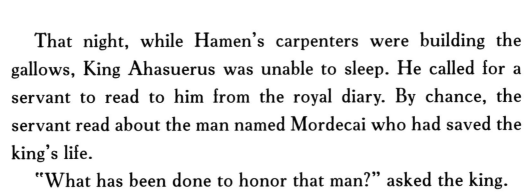

That night, while Hamen's carpenters were building the gallows, King Ahasuerus was unable to sleep. He called for a servant to read to him from the royal diary. By chance, the servant read about the man named Mordecai who had saved the king's life.

"What has been done to honor that man?" asked the king.

"Nothing at all," said the servant.

"Then we must do something immediately."

By coincidence, Hamen was in the courtyard waiting to get the king's permission to hang Mordecai.

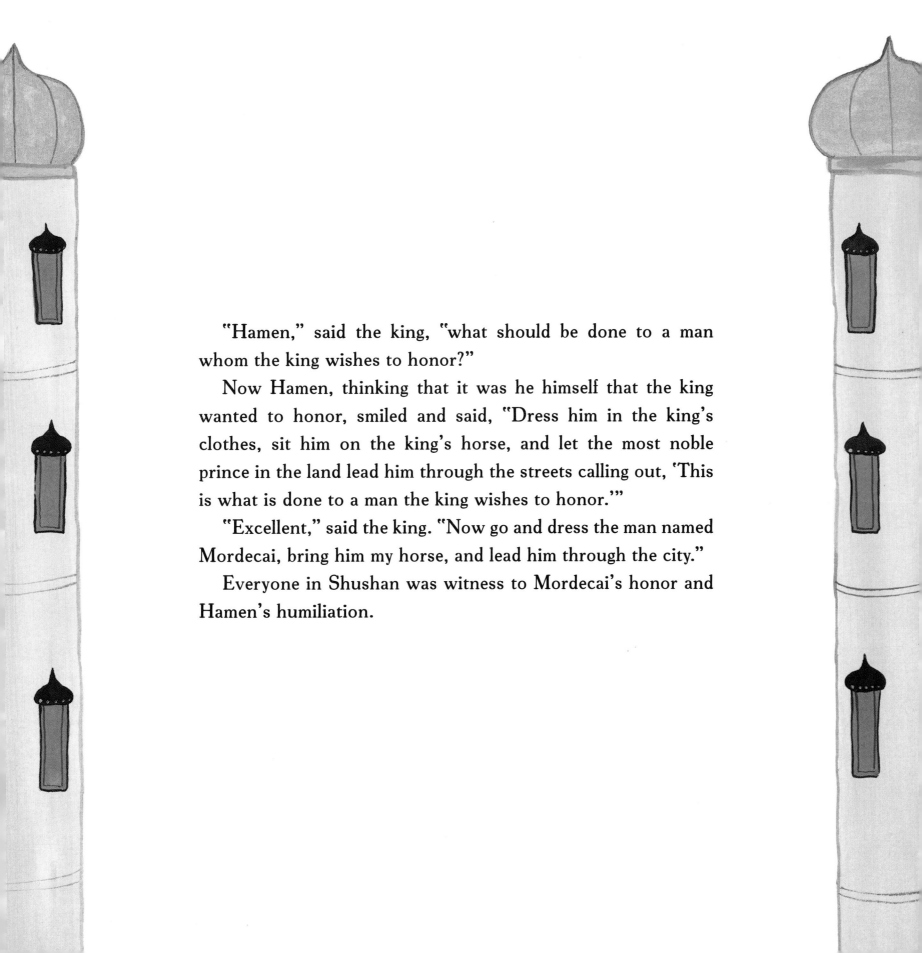

"Hamen," said the king, "what should be done to a man whom the king wishes to honor?"

Now Hamen, thinking that it was he himself that the king wanted to honor, smiled and said, "Dress him in the king's clothes, sit him on the king's horse, and let the most noble prince in the land lead him through the streets calling out, 'This is what is done to a man the king wishes to honor.'"

"Excellent," said the king. "Now go and dress the man named Mordecai, bring him my horse, and lead him through the city."

Everyone in Shushan was witness to Mordecai's honor and Hamen's humiliation.

That very night was the second banquet. Once again, when dessert was finished, the king asked Queen Esther what it was that she wanted.

"I ask that you save my life and the lives of my people," said the queen, "for it has been ordered that we are all to be destroyed."

"Who has ordered such a thing?" asked the king. "Who is this enemy of our people?"

"Our enemy, sire, is Hamen."

The king jumped up in rage.

Within hours, Hamen was hanged on the gallows he had built for Mordecai. And on the thirteenth day of Adar, it was not the Jews who died, but their enemies.

Jews throughout Persia rejoiced and celebrated.

Mordecai became the prime minister. One of his first decrees was that Jews everywhere, every year, celebrate the holiday of Purim on the fourteenth and fifteenth days of Adar, the days when sorrow turned into joy.

As for King Ahasuerus, he continued to be vain and foolish and hot-tempered. And he was still too busy drinking and eating to think about his kingdom.

But now, instead of Hamen's evil, it was the wisdom of Mordecai and his cousin Queen Esther that ruled the Persian Empire.

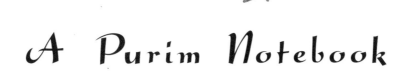

A Purim Notebook

The story of Esther is written on a scroll called the Megillah. On the fourteenth (or fifteenth) day of the Hebrew month of Adar (usually during the month of March), the Megillah is read in the synagogue. Every time the name Hamen is said, people make noise, stamp their feet, shout, hiss, or twirl noisemakers called *gragers*. *Yimah shmo*, may his name be erased . . . or in this case, drowned out.

Purim calls for creativity. In addition to hissing, booing, and shouting, some people make noise by putting nails in a cookie tin, by writing Hamen on the bottom of their shoes and stamping, and by writing his name on balloons . . . and popping them to drown out that evil name.

The Megillah says that Hamen had ten sons. When the reader reads the Megillah, the names of all ten are read without taking a breath: Parshandatha and Dalphon and Aspatha and Paratha and Adalia and Aridatha and Parmashta and Arisai and Aridai and Vaizatha.

Esther is a Persian name which means "star." Esther's Hebrew name is Hadassah, which is the name of a beautiful tree with sweet-smelling white flowers.

When Hamen chose the date on which the Jews were to die, he drew "lots," that is, he chose the day by lottery. The word Purim means lots.

Purim is a holiday of joy and abandon. It's a time to break rules and get rid of inhibitions. Also it is a custom on Purim for people to bring gifts of food to their friends, and food and money to the poor.

In synagogues all over the world there are masquerade parties on Purim . . . and carnivals. The word for a Purim carnival is *adloyada,* which means "until you can't tell the difference." People are supposed to be so crazy and so wild that they can't tell the difference between Ahasuerus and Hamen.

The word God does not appear once in the Book of Esther, perhaps because the turning back of the enemy was accomplished by Esther and Mordecai and not by miracles of God. Or, perhaps, because the reading of the Megillah gets so noisy and wild, that the writer of the Book of Esther thought it would be more respectful to leave the name of God out.

In Israel on Purim, people march through the streets in costume and bonk each other over the head with plastic hammers, just for fun.

It has been told in one of the Bible's commentaries that Hamen's daughter saw her father leading Mordecai through the city and thought, from above, that Mordecai was the one leading the horse. She emptied a chamberpot on her father's head, thinking he was Mordecai!

Today, in Jerusalem, Purim is observed on the fifteenth of Adar because that's when the Jews of Shushan observed the holiday. Everywhere else, it is observed on the fourteenth.

One of the most popular Purim foods is the Hamentashen — a three-cornered pastry (like Hamen's hat) usually stuffed with prunes or poppyseed.

Purim comes to an end with a Purim meal called a *seudah*, where family and friends eat together. Often there are plays about Queen Esther at the *seudah*.

The lesson of Purim: People should be able to live as they wish . . . as long as they don't hurt anybody.